The Beau Street Hoard

Eleanor Ghey

The British Museum

The Beau Street Hoard

Silver coins, smooth and weighty, were counted into piles by careful hands. They chinked as they were scooped off the table into a soft leather bag and placed with the others. As the footsteps retreated, the coins lay in their dark corner, packed in by stones and hidden from view…

© 2014 The Trustees of the British Museum

Eleanor Ghey has asserted the right to be identified as the author of this work

First published in 2014 by
The British Museum Press
A division of The British Museum
Company Ltd
38 Russell Square
London WC1B 3QQ

britishmuseum.org/publishing

A catalogue record for this book is available from the British Library
ISBN: 978-0-7141-1826-0

Designed by James Alexander
at Jade Design
Printed in China by SC (Sang Choy)
International Pte Ltd.

Front cover: A group of silver coins from the hoard. © The Trustees of the British Museum
Back cover: Silver radiate of Gordian III. © The Trustees of the British Museum

The British Museum

LOTTERY FUNDED

V&A Purchase Grant Fund

THE HEADLEY TRUST

Bath & North East Somerset Council

THE GAINSBOROUGH
BATH SPA

Contents

1 · Unearthing the hoard

How was the hoard discovered?

The first glimpse of the Beau Street hoard came when archaeologists at a Bath city-centre building site noticed a scattering of loose coins. It was November 2007 and Cotswold Archaeology was carrying out excavations in advance of construction of The Gainsborough Bath Spa Hotel on a plot between Lower Borough Walls and Beau Street.

Suspecting the presence of more coins, the archaeologists used a metal detector and found a strong signal nearby, suggesting that many more coins might be present. Sure enough, as excavation progressed, Hazel O'Neill, one of Cotswold Archaeology's site staff, was able to reveal a substantial hoard. The mass of fused coins lay in a right angle created between the walls of a Roman building (probably the corner of a room). It was tightly packed in on the other sides by two stones, forming a stone-lined chamber.

Left A close up of the coins as they were discovered.
Below The discovery of the hoard.
Below right The hoard being prepared for lifting.

The archaeologists decided to lift the hoard as a block with its surrounding soil so that it could be excavated under laboratory conditions. Once the full extent of the hoard was established and its position accurately planned and recorded, it was surrounded by supporting materials and placed into a wooden crate, before being lifted from the site by crane.

Did the hoard count as Treasure?

At this stage, the exact contents of the hoard were still unknown, but the weight and size of the block suggested a large number of coins. It had been clear from the moment of discovery that the hoard was

Left The site in Bath before redevelopment, seen from the Lower Borough Walls side.
Right The hoard being lifted from the site. It weighed 120kg with its packaging.

likely to qualify as Treasure under the 1996 Treasure Act, as it was
a large group of coins over 300 years old from the same find. The
numismatist Richard Reece studied a small sample and found it to
be largely silver Roman coins from the third century AD. To count
as Treasure there would need to be only two or more silver coins
(or ten or more base-metal coins). Under UK law, such hoards are
considered to be the property of the Crown though in practice the
Treasure Act allows interested museums to buy them through a set
process.

As the Roman Baths in Bath hoped to acquire the coins, an
inquest was held in June 2008 at which the hoard was duly declared
to be Treasure. The Treasure process could not then go any further
until the coins had been fully excavated from the block and cleaned
to a level that would allow identification. The British Museum's
statutory role in this process is to provide a report on the contents
of the hoard so that two independent experts (usually auctioneers)
can value it. The valuation is considered by the Treasure Valuation
Committee, who then sets the price to be paid by the acquiring
museum, subject to agreement by all parties. Usually, the money
is split between the finder of the Treasure and the landowner in
question, but in this case the finders were professional archaeologists
and therefore ineligible to receive a share.

2 · At the British Museum

What was in the soil block?

The hoard was brought to the British Museum where conservators in the metals section of the Museum's Department of Conservation and Scientific Research carried out a preliminary assessment. Pippa Pearce, the senior conservator who led this work, loosened some coins from the surface of the soil block. Intriguingly, these appeared to be base-metal coins of the sort more commonly found in a late third-century AD hoard rather than the silver coins that Richard Reece had identified previously. Everyone was keen to find out what was actually in the hoard.

In order to plan for its excavation and conservation the Museum needed to estimate the number of coins in the soil block and how densely they were packed within it. This proved problematic because the block was too big and dense for the Museum's own X-ray machine.

Unloading the hoard at the University of Southampton.

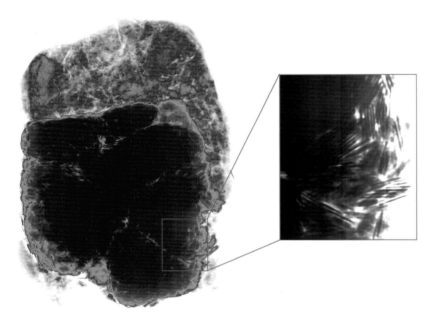

The X-ray showing separate bags of coins. The enlarged box shows individual coins tightly packed together.

By happy chance, the Museum was approached around this time by the University of Southampton's Department of Engineering Sciences which was developing a new imaging technology at the μ-VIS CT Imaging Centre. The University's Department of Archaeology was keen to test the application of this technique on archaeological finds and it had already used it with great success on two other coin hoards contained within ceramic vessels. Unfortunately, the soil block proved too heavy for this new equipment, but the Department kindly offered to X-ray it and produced a high-quality image of the contents of the hoard.

The resulting X-radiograph caused great excitement at the British Museum and in Bath. It revealed that the block was made up of clearly defined bags of coins, in at least six separate packages. It was even possible to see that the coins appeared to be of different sizes in different areas of the hoard, although the exact contents remained subject to speculation. There seemed to be no sign of box-fittings or other objects associated with the coins. This image allowed conservator Julia Tubman to begin to plan how she would approach the removal of the coins from the block.

How was the hoard conserved?

Once the hoard was back in the British Museum conservation laboratory, the process of excavating the coins began. Although the X-ray image showed distinctly separate masses of coins within the block, conditions of preservation can vary greatly. There was no guarantee that it would be possible to make out the divisions between the different masses in reality.

Julia starting to excavate the hoard in the laboratory.

However, as Julia began to remove the soil, working with the X-ray as a guide, it quickly became clear that the individual bags could be located. This was made easier because a thin reddish-brown layer of organic material still divided the bags from each other. Although greatly decayed, this was thought to be the remains of leather or textile, still preserved after nearly two thousand years in the soil. This remarkable result meant that the hoard could now be treated as not just one single mass of coins, but as a number of

Nearing the end of the excavation of the hoard. The division between the two bags is clearly visible.

The surviving organic material surrounding a bag of coins, visible as an orange/brown layer.

individual hoards within the same deposit. Julia and her colleagues decided to excavate these in sequence and assess their contents separately, to see if they differed.

The next surprise was that the first coins revealed by Julia were larger, higher in silver content and consequently better preserved than those in the sample taken by Pippa. After gentle cleaning they displayed an attractive silver surface and were revealed to be silver coins from the middle of the third century AD, rather than the smaller late third-century base-metal coins more commonly found in Romano-British hoards. Given the presence of a concentration of these coins and the two very different samples taken previously, it was starting to look like the hoard had been separated out into bags containing coins of different dates.

As excavation of the hoard progressed, the divisions between the bags remained distinct. Their position within the block was carefully recorded and the coins from each bag were kept together. As the final bags were removed, it became apparent that the coins had been placed directly onto the ground (or floor) surface, which was slightly concave in the centre of the block (possibly from the weight of the coins). A thin piece of partly mineralized wood was found at the base of the block, but this was fragmentary and not part of a box containing the hoard. The bags of coins had been piled together in the corner of the room and wedged in with stones to keep them together.

The excavation of the hoard was documented by the conservator as it progressed, and time lapse photography was also set up to capture this unrepeatable event. When all but one bag had been removed, the oval shape of the final bag could clearly be seen. It was being held together by the corrosion of the copper and silver in the coins. Although the Museum curators were keen to count and study the contents of this bag, they also wanted to preserve its appearance for display purposes and so a 3D scan was made to record its shape. To do this, an image of the bag was taken from all angles, allowing a computer to reconstruct the dimensions, surface and even the colour of the bag in a three-dimensional 'printout'.

Samples were taken of the organic material surrounding the money bags for identification under a scanning electron microscope. Close examination of the fibres within the material confirmed that it was a skin product. The material was greatly decayed and it was not possible to be sure if the skin had been tanned to create leather, or whether it was an untanned skin or hide. Under exceptional conditions of preservation, it is sometimes possible to identify from which animal the skin came, but so far this has not been the case here.

Left The final bag remaining. **Right** Coins before (right) and after cleaning (left).

Although organic material decays in the ground over long periods, it is likely that it was partially preserved by the coins themselves. Copper minerals leaching out of the corroding coins created a microenvironment that was toxic to the bacteria that cause decay.

The final stage in the conservation process was separating and cleaning the individual coins. Some were covered in a hard brown layer of corrosion and soil that made it difficult to see their inscriptions and designs. Gentle manual and chemical cleaning under the microscope allowed these details to be read and the coins to be identified by the British Museum's coin curators.

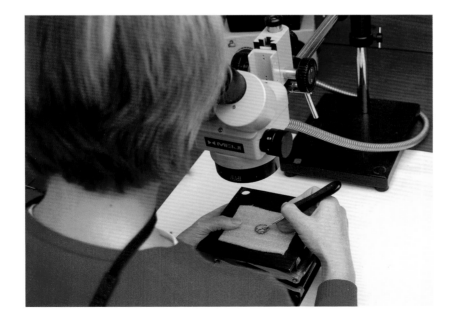

A coin being manually cleaned under the microscope in the conservation laboratory.

A *denarius* of Mark Antony, the oldest coin in the hoard (32–31 BC).

A *denarius* of Severus Alexander (AD 222–35).

What did the hoard contain?

It was now the task of the Museum's Department of Coins and Medals to sort and identify the coins. A summary of the contents of each bag was prepared, with the numbers of each denomination of coin and the number issued by each Roman emperor recorded. Typically, a hoard will consist of a variety of coins of different dates that circulated at the same time in the past, just as today the change in our pocket will include both recent and older coins. In the third century AD, emperors tended to reign for relatively short periods but their coins continued to be used for some time afterwards. Coins were eventually removed from circulation when the newer coinage was significantly lower in silver content and less valuable than the older coins (in the same way that modern British copper coins have been gradually replaced by copper plated steel, due to the rising value of copper). This process allows coin experts (numismatists) to date a hoard, with the overall composition suggesting the period in which the coins circulated. The most recently issued coin in the hoard suggests a more precise date after which the hoard is likely to have been buried.

The hoard contained over 17,500 Roman coins; the majority were found in eight separate bags of coins (see the table on page 21), but there was also a number of loose coins that had spilled out of the bags where the material holding them fast had decayed. The eight bags can be put into three groups as follows.

1. One bag of *denarii* dating up to the AD 250s.

The *denarius* (plural *denarii*) is usually distinguished by the laurel wreath worn by the emperor on the obverse ('head') side of the coin.

The earliest coin in the hoard was a much worn *denarius* of Mark Antony, issued in the final years of the Roman Republic in 32–31 BC (that is, about 300 years before its eventual burial). These are relatively common in British hoards even into the third century AD. Other Roman Republican and early Imperial *denarii* with a higher silver content were removed from circulation and recycled, but this particular issue contained less silver and so continued in use for centuries. The latest *denarius* in the bag was issued by the emperor Gordian III (AD 238–44) but the bag also contained a handful of radiates, the latest of which dated to the AD 250s.

A silver radiate of Gordian III (AD 238–44).

2. Four bags of silver radiates dating up to the AD 260s.

The coins known to us as 'radiates' (from the spiked rays shown on the head of the emperor in imitation of the sun god, Sol) were issued from the earlier third century AD, when they probably had a value twice that of the *denarius*. They were visibly larger in size than the *denarius* at that time and were mostly silver. These bags were among the largest in size from the hoard, but also included one much smaller bag. This indicates that either the bags were not made up to a standard size or weight, or perhaps that this bag was yet to be filled.

3. Three bags of base-metal radiates dating up to the AD 270s.

These radiates date to a later period (AD 260s–270s), by which time the silver content of the coins issued had decreased to the point where they were essentially bronze. They are smaller and more corroded. At this time the Roman Empire was in crisis and the breakaway Gallic empire issued its own coins. The issues of the

Gallic emperors Postumus, Victorinus and Tetricus I and II are among the most common Roman coins found in Britain and their cruder appearance reflects the vast quantities produced.

The contents of the hoard:

	Silver radiates	Bronze radiates	Denarii	Total	Date of latest coin (AD)
Bag 1	**3737**	44	22	3803	272–274
Bag 2	84	**2947**	2	3033	272–274
Bag 3	**2668**	97	8	2773	271–274
Bag 4	**2270**	6	26	2302	260–269
Bag 5	**747**	15	13	775	260–269
Bag 6	24	0	**1771**	1795	253–260
Bag 7	20	**386**	0	406	272–274
Bag 8	5	**247**	1	253	272–274
Loose coins				2437	
Hoard total				17577	

A base-metal radiate of the Gallic emperor Tetricus II (AD 272–4).

3 · Understanding and interpreting the hoard

When was it buried?

The most recent coins in the three bags of base-metal radiates were issued in AD 271 to 274, in the names of the emperor Tetricus I and his son Tetricus II, making them the latest in the hoard. These coins were produced in very large numbers and are extremely common in late third-century hoards from Britain. However, there were relatively few of them in the latest bags of the Beau Street hoard. It is therefore likely that the hoard was buried (or at least no longer added to) during these years, because if it had been buried slightly later we would expect a larger number of these issues to have built up.

There are a number of possible scenarios for the deposition of the hoard. It may have been buried all at once in the AD 270s after being sorted into separate bags, possibly containing coins gathered from another location, such as an offering in a spring or temple. Or the collection of bags of coins may have been formed gradually, with the cache being added to over time as savings were amassed. It is certainly the case that by the time the final bag of coins was filled the earlier coins were no longer in general use, having been removed from the circulating supply due to their higher silver content. They might have been kept in anticipation of future use or for their weight in precious metal. The most recent coins from these

The Piercebridge ploughman, wearing the *birrus Britannicus*.

earlier bags show little surface wear, suggesting that they did not circulate for long before they joined the hoard. Either way, this was a hoard that was built up over several decades before it reached its final composition.

What was it worth in Roman times?

The AD 270s were a time of instability in the Roman Empire, with inflation fuelling rapidly rising prices. This, together with the lack of historical records, makes it difficult to say how much the coin hoard was worth in real terms. Although the early silver radiates can be assumed to be worth roughly two silver *denarii*, there is no information about the comparative value of the copper alloy radiates issued from the AD 260s. Indeed, they do not appear to have had an officially recognized relationship to silver and gold, although their face value was probably higher than their value as bullion. However, reforms to the coinage by the emperor Aurelian in AD 274 meant that these older base-metal radiates probably became almost worthless in official transactions, although it is likely that they were still acceptable as small change in Britain for many years after that.

Information about the cost of items in the Roman world is given in inscriptions of the Edict on Maximum Prices issued by the emperor Diocletian in AD 301. These use the *denarius* as a unit of account. For example, a day's wage for an agricultural or manual labourer has the maximum tariff of 25 *denarii* while the *birrus Britannicus*, a hooded woollen cloak from Britain (opposite), could cost up to 6,000 *denarii*. However, by this time the coinage had been reformed again and new denominations issued, so these prices cannot be assumed to be the same as those of thirty years earlier. It is also unwise to assume that these prices, drawn up by officials in Rome, bore any relation to those in the markets of Roman Britain. It is likely that exchange and barter systems were also in operation, and soldiers in the army would probably have received a proportion of their pay in kind.

The problem of applying this to the hoard can be seen if we try to estimate the value of one of the bags. The largest bag in the hoard contained 3,737 silver radiates and 22 *denarii* (ignoring a few copper alloy radiates). This gives a total value of silver coins in the bag of approximately 7,496 *denarii* using the 2 *denarii* to a radiate ratio thought to have been current in AD 230. This would equate to about 300 days' wages if we take the AD 301 maximum figure of 25 *denarii* a day, but by then these coins were unlikely to have been officially in use. They are likely, however, to have had some value based on the silver content of the coins. In AD 301 a pure silver coin was decreed to have a value of 100 *denarii*. These coins would have contained between 25–30 per cent silver, giving an upper estimate of value as high as 94,000 to 188,000 *denarii*, or 3,760 to 7,520 days' wages. Their purchasing power in the intervening periods of inflation and monetary reform can only be guessed at. That said, it is one of the larger hoards of its period from Roman Britain and so must surely have represented a considerable sum of money.

What do we know about Roman Bath?
We will never know exactly why the hoard was buried or why it was not recovered. But one way to try to understand the nature of the hoard is to look at the place in which it was found.

At the heart of Bath is the Roman temple complex dedicated to the goddess Sulis Minerva. The baths within this complex are built around and fed by a sacred spring, one of three naturally occurring hot springs in the town. Pre-Roman activity at this sacred spring

The Cross Bath, etching
by John Fayram 1738.

Drawing of the King's Bath and the Queen's Bath in Bath, 1675 by Thomas Johnson.

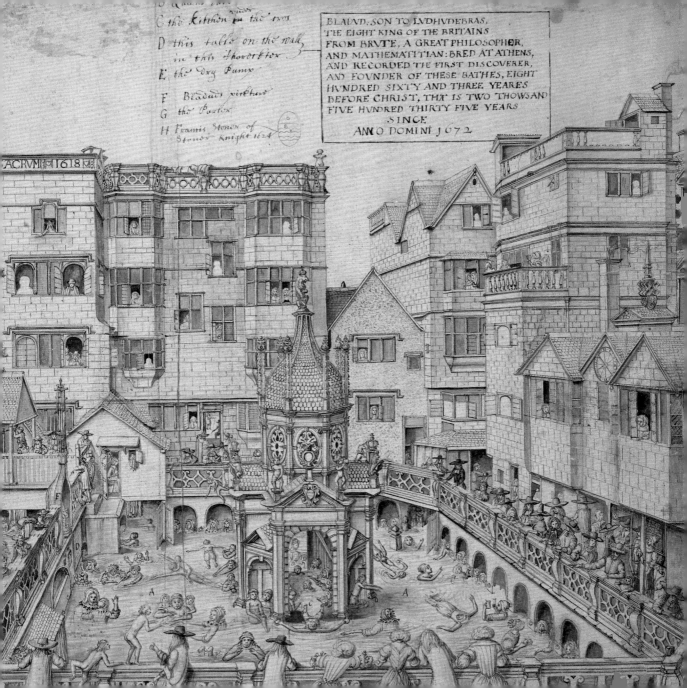

B Queens bath
C the Kitchin in the cros
D this table on the wall
in this thorowfar
E the dry Pumx
F Bladuds virthow
G the Poolox
H Frauns Stoner of
Stoner Knight 1624

BLADUD, SON TO LUDHUDEBRAS,
THE EIGHT KING OF THE BRITAINS
FROM BRUTE, A GREAT PHILOSOPHER,
AND MATHEMATITIAN: BRED AT ATHENS,
AND RECORDED THE FIRST DISCOVERER,
AND FOVNDER OF THESE BATHES, EIGHT
HVNDRED SIXTY AND THREE YEARES
BEFORE CHRIST, THAT IS TWO THOWSAND
FIVE HVNDRED THIRTY FIVE YEARS
SINCE
ANNO DOMINI 1672

ACRVM 1618

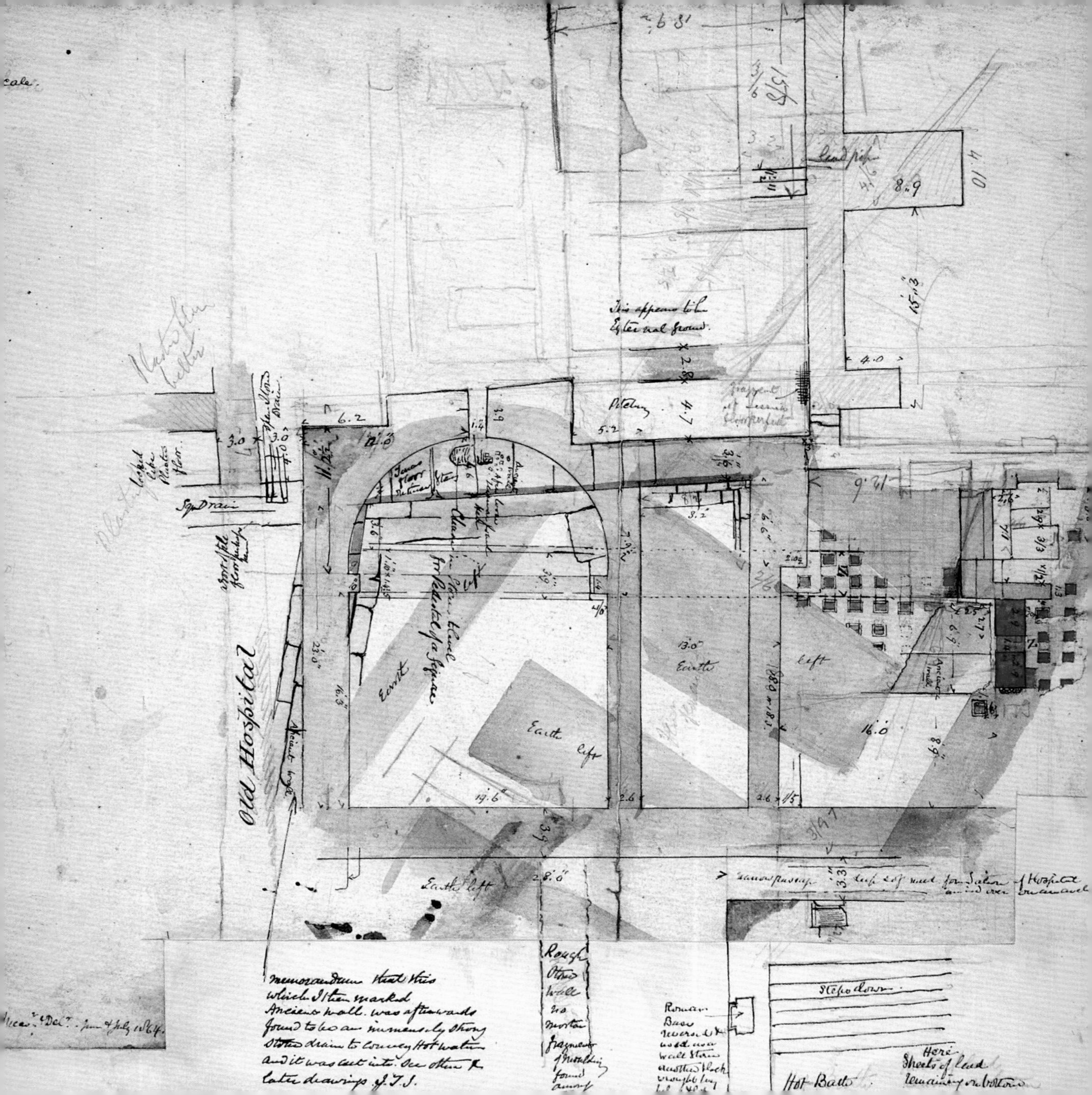

Scale.

Old Hospital

This appears to be
External ground.

lead pipe

Sy Drain

It appears to be
External ground.

Etching

Fragment of
ancient
counterfeit

6.2

3.0   3.0

Earth

Earth left

13.0"
Earth

left

16.0

Earth left

Earth left

Ancient
wall

19.6

2.6   15

Narrow passage   left 2 of wall for Sakar of Hospital
carried over drain level

Rough
Other
Wall
no
mortar
fragment
of moulding
found
among

Roman
Base
reversed &
would now
would form
another block
would lay
old wall

Steps down

Hot Baths

Here
Sheets of lead
remaining on bottom

Memorandum that this
which I then marked
Ancient wall. was afterwards
found to be an immensely strong
stone drain to convey Hot water
and it was cut into. See other &
later drawings J.T.S.

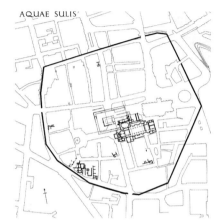

Left Plan of the Roman buildings excavated in 1864. The findspot of the hoard lay to the south east (upper left of this image).
Above top Map of the known archaeological remains of Roman Bath, showing the city walls. The red dot indicates the findspot of the hoard.
Above The Roman baths today.

is shown by finds of Iron Age coins but it was during the Roman period that the elaborate buildings surrounding it were constructed. It then became a focus for ritual offerings, including thousands of coins thrown into the water. Later, the King's Bath was built over the spring. Two other springs are located to the southwest of this complex, near the area in which the hoard was found. They were also the focus of later medieval bathing establishments known as the Hot Bath and the Cross Bath. The former was connected to a Roman bath house and the Cross Bath spring was also a focus for activity in the Roman period.

The hoard was found in a block of land about 150 metres southwest of the main temple complex. The excavated area in which it was found lies below the nineteenth-century foundations of the Gainsborough building, formerly the Royal United Hospital (and later a college). Excavations in the 1860s by the archaeologist James Irvine prior to the construction of an extension to this hospital revealed a Roman bathing complex that was probably associated with the spring known as the Hot Bath. The Beau Street hoard was placed in a pit cut through the upper layer of a sequence of floors in a Roman building that lay to the east of the apsidal bath excavated by Irvine (separated from it by a corridor). He also uncovered a building with a hypocaust floor and mosaic, separated from these baths by a gravelled street.

Little is known about the function of the buildings uncovered by Irvine, but their rich decoration and size suggests a bathing establishment of some importance, possibly intended for public use rather than being for a private residence. Altars found in the area of the Hot Bath (and the Cross Bath, slightly to the north) suggest that this part of Bath might also have had a religious function. The altar set up by a son of Novantius following a 'vision' (on display in the

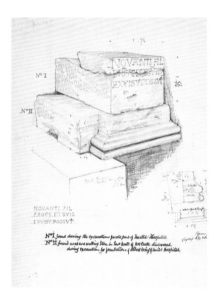

Roman Baths) comes from this part of the site, but it may have been reused here as building material; its base was incorporated into the east wall of a lead-lined bath in the complex excavated by Irvine and its upper part was found during construction work in the 1820s. It is clear that there were a number of phases of building on the site, and that the baths excavated by Irvine overlay earlier structures.

Left Drawing of the mosaic uncovered by Irvine.
Above Drawing by Irvine of the altar set up by a son of Novantius.
Right Photo of the altar now on display in the Roman Baths.

Head of the goddess Sulis
Minerva found below Stall
Street in 1727.

The nature of the immediate context in which the hoard was buried is of great importance for our interpretation of it, but so too is understanding the function of the Roman town. Apart from the extensively excavated temple complex, the Roman occupation of Bath as a whole is relatively poorly understood, partly due to the built-up nature of the modern city. During the Roman period a wall seems to have been built around the town, enclosing an area of about 10 hectares. This is small for a Roman town and unusually the area within these walls does not appear to have been densely occupied. It certainly seems unusual to have two substantial sets of baths in such close proximity.

Given the significant amount of space devoted to the temple complex, it is possible to view the entire area within the walls as a sacred precinct, rather than a conventional Roman town. Similar

Photograph of J. T. Irvine's 1864 excavations.

temple complexes excavated in Gaul contain a variety of structures: temples and smaller shrines, bath houses, sometimes theatres and other buildings possibly intended to provide accommodation and services to visitors. The evidence for occupation at such a site can therefore include activities that do not immediately appear to have a 'ritual' function, such as the preparation of food and metalworking. It is possible to imagine a thriving town growing up around the springs, with many opportunities for commercial activity.

We do not know to what extent this activity was overseen by the authorities in charge of the temple complex, although we know that

The excavation of the sacred spring in 1979.

Above Reconstruction of Bath in the Roman period.
Right Coins from the sacred spring.

temples were wealthy institutions in the Roman world. Money was given for their construction and maintenance by individuals seeking both to demonstrate their piety and to earn public esteem. The hoard suggests a degree of organization in the sorting and storage of a large sum of money. It may have belonged to an official connected to the temple or a wealthy individual attracted by the opportunities it presented. Unfortunately this has to remain speculation because at the moment we are not certain whether the building it was deposited in was a public one (part of a larger bathing complex, for example) or a private one (such as a house or business). As the archaeology of Bath continues to be uncovered our understanding of this unusual town will grow.

Fresco from the *Praedia* of Julia Felix in Pompeii.

The Magerius mosaic.

What is the significance of the Beau Street hoard?

Perhaps the most remarkable feature of the Beau Street hoard is that it contained separate money bags. We already know that Roman coins were sometimes stored and transported in bags. A fresco from Pompeii (opposite) shows coins bagged up and sorted by value alongside writing materials, perhaps for keeping accounts. The Magerius mosaic from Tunisia depicts a figure carrying a tray of four bags, each marked with the symbol for one thousand. These presumably contained the set sum of 1,000 *denarii* each and represent payment for the gladiatorial spectacles shown, including bonuses of 500 *denarii* per beast slaughtered, the inscription tells us. However it does not seem that the individual bags in the Bath hoard contained similar numbers of coins, or similar weights of silver, although it is difficult to be certain of the original weight of the bags. The uppermost bag had decayed and burst, scattering its contents and not all the loose coins can be assigned to a particular bag.

It is unusual for organic material to survive in hoards, but improvements in recovery methods and conservation techniques have produced a few examples from recent years. Traces of textile were found within a pot containing a fourth-century AD hoard from the Shrewsbury area. This suggests that the coins may have been wrapped in separate fabric bags before being placed in the pot. Indeed, when the coins were removed from the pot in layers, the upper few layers contained later coins that were absent in the lower layers, suggesting that they had been added to the pot over a decade

Above Preserved Roman textile from the Shrewsbury hoard.
Left The Frome hoard being excavated.

later. It may therefore be more common than previously suspected for a hoard to have built up over a long period of time.

Internal layering has also been identified in the Frome hoard, but this hoard was deposited in one single event. Although it is still being studied, preliminary results suggest that the most recent coins were clustered part of the way down the pot, and not at the top as one might expect. This and the way in which the coins lay inside the pot strongly indicate that the large pot was filled from the contents of a number of smaller containers before being buried. Unlike the Beau Street hoard, the coins from Frome were almost all of the same type, base-metal radiates, and likely to have been circulating at the same time.

How does it compare with other hoards from Roman Britain?

Hoards of base-metal radiates from the later third century AD are particularly common in Roman Britain. We still do not know exactly

Rock relief from Bishapur, Iran showing the capture of Roman emperors by the Sasanian emperor Shapur I.

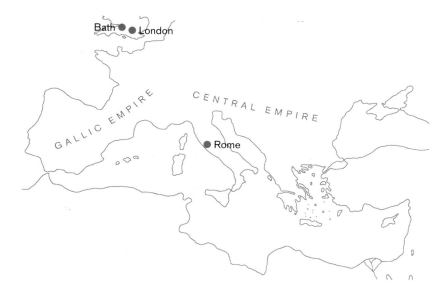

why this is but it is likely that a number of factors were involved, including a general background of political instability and inflation followed by monetary reforms.

Traditionally, the increase in the number of hoards buried has been linked to the insecurity of the times. The authority of the emperors in Rome had been weakened by warfare and barbarian incursions. The Sasanian empire was expanding from its base in modern Iran at this time and came into conflict with Rome in Syria and Mesopotamia. The emperors Philip I and Gordian were both defeated in the East by the Sasanian King Shapur I, and Valerian died whilst his captive in AD 260. Although Valerian's son Gallienus ruled in Rome, the western empire was vulnerable to a series of usurpers and in AD 260 the general

Postumus took control of what was effectively a breakaway empire in the West, ruling from northern Gaul and the Rhineland.

At its peak, this 'Gallic' empire encompassed the whole of Gaul, Britain and Spain. Until it was reincorporated by Aurelian in AD 274, the Gallic empire issued its own coinage in large quantities. Even after this period, Britain seems to have remained somewhat vulnerable to raiders from the continent, as possibly indicated by the building of walls around many towns and some new coastal forts. However, the extent to which this affected the Romano-British economy is uncertain; an increase in the size and number of villas at this time could suggest its relative prosperity when compared to the continent.

When looking at hoarding, it is difficult to disentangle these political factors from economic ones. In the years after AD 274, coin supply to Britain seems to have been unreliable, something we know from the great increase in local copies of official coinage. The new, higher value coinage issued by Aurelian may not have been plentiful or of low enough value to meet daily needs, but the old coinage is unlikely to have been suitable for official payments. Inflation rendered it almost worthless and it is easy to see how it might have ended up being discarded. The wide availability and low face value of these coins would also have made them a suitable offering to give to the gods. We know that the sacred spring in Bath attracted a great many offerings during this period, suggesting that Bath was still an important religious centre.

The Beau Street hoard does not resemble the typical hoard of this date found in Britain. These are usually somewhat smaller, ranging from several hundred coins up to a few thousand and are often buried in a ceramic container.

The mix of coins in the Beau Street hoard also appears highly

Key

✚ Coin hoard mentioned in text
● Late Roman provincial capitals

Hadrian's Wall

● York

✚ Normanby

✚ Shrewsbury

Beau Street
✚ ✚ Cunetio
✚ Frome

London
●

Dorchester
✚

Left Map of late third-century Roman Britain showing Bath, provincial capitals and coin hoards mentioned in the text. **Right** Coins from the Cunetio hoard.

unusual if we compare it with other larger hoards. The largest coin hoard from Roman Britain to date was found just outside the later walled area of the Roman town of Cunetio, near Mildenhall in Wiltshire in 1978. This contained 54,951 coins in a large ceramic jar and a lead box. The largest in a single container is the Frome hoard of 52,503 coins, discovered by a metal detectorist in Somerset in 2010. Both these hoards were largely made up of base-metal radiates (although there was also a small group of *denarii* in the Cunetio hoard). We will never know if the coins in the Cunetio hoard had originally been sorted in a similar way because it was not excavated under laboratory conditions.

A better parallel for the Beau Street hoard might be another hoard found in an urban context, the centre of Dorchester (Roman Durnovaria) in 1936. The coins were found in three containers buried alongside each other: a bronze jug, a bronze basin and a wooden container. In total it contained over 22,000 coins, almost all silver radiates dating up to AD 260. Again, the distribution of the coins among the three vessels is not known but they are likely to have been in circulation together.

Hoards of third-century *denarii* and silver radiates are usually found separately. The latter are less common in hoards, possibly due to the value these coins retained as a source of silver; they could have been traded or melted down. One recent discovery of a smaller such hoard from Somerset is the 3,339 coins found in a pit on a Roman rural settlement in Yeovil in 2013. The presence of an adjacent metalworking hearth could indicate that these were destined to be recycled. Generally speaking, finds of earlier Roman coins are uncommon in Somerset and the area tends to be viewed as something of a backwater in this period, but there are isolated glimpses of prosperity as, for example, in the hoard of 9,238 *denarii* dating to AD 224 found at Shapwick Roman villa.

A medium sized hoard of radiates found in a pot from the York area.

4 · The hoard returns to Bath

Since the hoard's discovery in 2007 many people have been involved in its excavation, conservation and study. The hoard has travelled from Bath to Wiltshire (where it was stored for a while), Southampton and London, where part of it was on temporary display at the British Museum. The work carried out at the British Museum and in Bath involved many volunteers photographing and weighing the coins. This will result in a permanent record of the contents of the hoard, both as a published catalogue and on the Roman Baths' collections database, making it available for further study in the future.

The Roman Baths has bought the hoard so that it can be investigated and enjoyed by many more people and find a permanent home near the

Children at the launch of the Beau Street hoard appeal.

place where it was found. Here it will offer a glimpse of a previously untold chapter in Bath's history, and show how the story of Bath is still unfolding as new discoveries are made and interpreted. The Heritage Lottery Fund has supported the project with funding for activities surrounding the hoard involving schools and the local community.

The Gainsborough Bath Spa hotel on the site of the hoard is due to open in 2014. It is fitting that the site continues to attract visitors to Bath's thermal springs just as it did in Roman times.

Above A replica of a money bag being handled by Alford, a member of the Bath Ethnic Minority Senior Citizens' Association.
Right Volunteers recording the coins at Bath.

Further reading

R.A. Abdy (2002), *Romano-British Coin Hoards*. Shire Publications Ltd

E.M. Besley and R.F. Bland (1983), *The Cunetio Treasure: Roman Coinage of the Third century AD*. British Museum Press

R.F. Bland and A.M. Burnett eds (1998), *The Normanby hoard and Other Roman Coin Hoards*. British Museum Press

B. Cunliffe (1984), *Roman Bath Discovered*. Routledge & Kegan Paul

B. Cunliffe, and P. Davenport (1985), *The Temple of Sulis Minerva at Bath*. Oxford University Committee for Archaeology Monograph no. 7 (2 vols)

S. Moorhead, A. Booth and R. Bland (2010), *The Frome Hoard*. British Museum Press

S. Moorhead (2013), *A History of Roman Coinage in Britain*. Greenlight Publishing

R. Reece (2002), *The Coinage of Roman Britain*. Tempus

Image credits

All images are © The Trustees of the British Museum with the following exceptions:

pp. 8, 29 (below), 31 (below), 32, 35 (right), 46, 47 (below) © The Roman Baths, Bath and North East Somerset Council

pp. 6, 7 (left), 7 (right), 9 © Cotswold Archaeology

p. 12 © University of Southampton

p. 29 reproduced from Cunliffe, Barry W. and Davenport, P., (1985) *The temple of Sulis Minerva at Bath, Vol. 1.*, Oxford: University Committee for Archaeology, with kind permission from Barry W. Cunliffe

pp. 28, 30, 31 (above), reproduced by the kind permission of National Museums Scotland

p. 33 © Bath in Time - Bath Central Library

p. 34 © Bath in Time - Bath Preservation Trust (photograph by Lesley Green-Armytage)

p. 35 (left) courtesy of John Hodgson

p. 36 © Soprintendenza Speciale per I Beni archaeologici di Napoli e Pompei

p. 37 akg-images/Gilles Mermet

p. 38 © Somerset County Council

p. 39 © Georgina Herrmann

p. 47 (above) courtesy of Sandy Wu-Grant

Acknowledgements

Many people have been involved in the story of the Beau Street hoard to date. I would like to acknowledge the contribution made by the following. At the Roman Baths: Verity Anthony, Lindsey Braidley, Stephen Clews, Susan Fox, Saira Holmes and many volunteers past and present. My colleagues in the British Museum Department of Coins and Medals and Portable Antiquities and Treasure: Richard Abdy, Ben Alsop, Roger Bland, Henry Flynn, Ian Leins, Sam Moorhead, Emma Morris, Ian Richardson and Rachel Wilkinson; in the Department of Conservation and Scientific Research: Caroline Cartwright, Hazel Gardiner, Marilyn Hockey, Natalie Mitchell, Pippa Pearce, Ana Tam, Julia Tubman and also Mark Conway and Stephen Dodd from Collections Services; Emma Poulter, Axelle Russo-Heath and Alice White from British Museum Press and David Prudames for his help with the blog.

I would also like to thank Graeme Earl and Mark Mavrogordato (University of Southampton), Martin Watts (Cotswold Archaeology), Adrian Chadwick, Peter Cox and Emma Firth (AC Archaeology) and Paul Cox.

The project has been supported by thousands of individual donations from the public and with grants and donations from: Trevor Osborne Property Group (Bath Hotel and Spa Ltd); YTL Hotels (Gainsborough Bath Spa Hotel); Heritage Lottery Fund; Victoria & Albert Purchase Grant Fund; The Headley Trust; The Roman Society; The Association for Roman Archaeology and The UK Numismatic Trust.